The Wires: 2012

JUDE COWAN MONTAGUE

wisdom's bottom press

Published 2016
by Wisdom's Bottom Press

©2016 *Jude Cowan Montague*
Forward © 2016 *Line Hassall Thomsen*

All rights reserved. No part of this book may be reprinted, reproduced, stored, or utilised in any form, by any electronic, mechanical, or other means, now known or hereafter invented, including printing, photocopying, saving on disk, broadcasting, or recording, or in any information storage or retrieval system, other than for purposes of fair use, without written permission from the publishers.

Wisdom's Bottom Press
15 King's Road, St Leonards-on-Sea, TN37 6EA

e-mail: wisdoms.bottom@zoho.com
www: http://www.wisdomsbottom.com/

ISBN   978-0-9935502-1-8

Also by Jude Cowan Montague
For the Messengers (Donut Press, 2011)
The Groodoyals of Terre Rouge (Dark Windows Press, 2013)

Printed and bound by imprintdigital.com, Upton Pyne, Exeter

Acknowledgements
Many thanks to so many for their support but I am particularly grateful to the poets Kirsten Irving, Mark Waldron, Daniel Lehan, and Peter J. King for their help and input..

Dedication
For the Messengers

Contents

Foreword... 1

Author's Preface... 3

Signs.. 5

Coming.. 18

Beyond.. 40

Battle... 58

Settlement... 73

Foreword

"You are only as good as your next news story!" and; "the next news story is always the most important news story" – these were often repeated phrases when I worked in the newsrooms of I.T.V. News, BBC News and Channel 4 News. We news journalists rarely look back at news stories from yesterday or even from a few years back. And we rarely linger at details of stories that never made it to the news bulletin. This book proves that reflecting on details of yesterday's stories is not only useful but extremely relevant.

I first met Jude Cowan Montague in the atrium of the I.T.N. building at Gray's Inn Road in London. I was a news journalist, working for both *I.T.V. News* and *Channel 4 News*; she was an archivist at Reuters in the basement. We both had a passion for writing poetry. It was refreshing to meet another news worker and poet. During the long working days mixed with tsunamis, terror, tragedy and images too terrible to report, it was a breath of fresh air to stumble upon Cowan Montague and discuss the stories from another perspective.

After years of working in the newsroom I ventured to write a Ph.D. on news journalism culture while Cowan Montague embarked on a poetic study of the Reuters wires, with her first book For the Messengers published 2013. This book marks the second in her series of news poetry, and I very much hope it is not the last of its kind.

These days, when more and more news stories are constantly arriving on more and more media platforms, we need more than ever to stop up and reflect on the small details of life reported. For, as Cowan Montague shows on every page of this book, there are so many unreported details of life out there which makes the world come to life in ways which twenty-second soundbites just cannot. And while the countless news stories that flash before us in a day are often forgotten, the images and stories that Jude Cowan Montague presents us with in this book linger and stay in the mind.

Consider the lines (p. 24) describing a mother who has just lost her twelve-year-old daughter in a terror-filled country in the Middle East:

> Tears roll down tracks of cheeks into open pink mouth.
> Facebones ache from unwanted, uncontrollable hiccups.
> My twelve-year-old is carried high.
> Oh wow, she suddenly shot up, much taller than her mum.

> White lilies
> Daffodils
> Chrysanthemums

At times the prose and layout is playful, at times it is more traditional. Sometimes the poems are constructed on the page to suit their stories, like **23:16,** which illustrates both in words and layout the shuffling scene of an activist making tea.

Some of the themes of poems and text are mixed up. A description of an Olympic medal hopeful might be followed by a scene of children spurting towards a car, pointing a machine gun out of a window. To readers, this might seem confusing at first. But this indeed shows the very reality of life inside a newsroom which journalists and news archivists constantly have to work with.

New news and images constantly flash by; there is no constant theme except the Good News Story.

With concise words and sentences, Cowan Montague gives life and meaning to what a T.V.-news item might have condensed to a two-second flash with a voice-over.

Journalism, news and poetry are intrinsically linked. As with Cowan Montague's first collection of news wire poetry, this collection reminds me of the connections between journalism and poetry. Over one hundred years ago, in his essay *The Critic as Artist* (1890), Oscar Wilde quipped about the difference between literature and journalism: "Journalism is unreadable, and literature is not read".

Today, poetry is still largely unread by the public while news stories are consumed like never before. Arguably, the quality and depth of news stories is not made better by the increased use of social media. Rather, news of today has to be presented in an ever more short, sexy and snappy fashion. This kind of tabloidisation of the world has a tendency to turn real life tragedy into simple stories which users can quickly share on a Facebook newsfeed, on Instagram or Twitter. In this way, the very small details, the very life of news stories may get lost in the rush of current news. As this book in hand shows, a poem gives space and time for reflection, and a new human engagement in the story that no Facebook news item can do.

I believe that the best poetry is like a mirror which is held up to the world. The best journalism should also aim to hold up a mirror to the world. The ways of presenting may be different, but in my view, both disciplines could learn a lot from each other.

I hope you enjoy Jude Cowan Montague's poetic look at the wires of 2012!

Dr Line Hassall Thomsen
Journalist and poet, author of *New Struggles, Old Ideals* (2013)

Author's Preface

International television news is mediated for consumers by national and local broadcasters even within the current rise of internet journalism and social media.. This book deals with the mostly invisible process of television news-gathering that lies behind the programmes. It re-imagines Reuters edits catalogued in my job as an archivist for I.T.N. Source during 2012.

     I have divided my poetical collage into five sections. Although their titles suggest a narrative, I have roughly followed existing chronology, choosing no conscious theme and imposing no hierarchy. This process reflects the relatively unpackaged manner in which feeds arrive at a central hub.

Signs

00:02

In silent vigil –
for criminals are still free men
and the Coptic Church was scattered with body parts –
a girl holds a sign
depicting Jesus
but I don't recognise him

at the Santa Apolónia train station
with no trains –
or rather there are trains
but they won't move today

– in a state of depression.
"There is no lower than this.
It calls for endurance.
There is no lower than this."

The IRINN DOG flashes up stories in English and Arabic:
Bahraini Regime Troops kill 15-year-old protester in Sitra

00:35

"Under his wise leadership,"
      says the Agricultural Ministry director,
"modern pig,
     duck, and
         chickenfarms were built.
My resolution is to establish a ring-shaped,
  cyclic   production
   system   in obedience
     to the call of the joint
                      New Year editorial."

Makoto Hirata has handed himself in.
It's been sixteen years.
Where is the body of the chief clerk
who wanted his relative to leave the cult?
The son of the missing wears a red jumper
and wants to know everything.

02:27

El Brujo has returned; our dear mayor dispenses predictions.
His kindly face scans journalists who kneel before the future.
"President Obama will lose, because he has expelled more Latinos
from the US than anyone else in history."
Reporters must undergo purification rites.
                    By the way, any forecast
can be changed, at any time, by magical spells.

Big Sky Politics.
        Our hands are dirty, but your smile is clean;
        why wait any longer for the one you love?
                The lady must appear in person,
            not only on notebooks.

03.52

Father found out about their son's death on Facebook.
Politician: "It must be so hard for you."
Mother wipes her eyes with the heel of her hand once,
                                                    twice,
                                                    three times,
impossible not to cry when someone's being nice to you.

Three ate it.
                A little bitter perhaps,
                so two stopped while the millionaire
                carried on.
        A stripped carcass balances on stiff pads
resting on thick circles of wood by a shiny cleaver.
Long
            intestines
                    trail
                        away
                                  past the pink plastic bowl.
It was *gelsemium elegans* that was popped
in the pot.
                "I thought they hadn't cleaned the cat properly,"
                explains Huang,
                who no longer has paralysis of the throat.

The carpet of anger
cannot be crossed
by the videographer
who reels before
the wave
of sound and spittle.

The people do want to execute you, Bashar!

06:02

Black smoke. Brisk waves. Scott Smiles seizes the radio beacon, pockets his wallet, yanks the Esky. Leaps. "Boys got their life jackets on?" Check. Clinging to a cooler box four bob along the coast.

Riley Smiles, he's eleven, shakes his head, pokes his chin with middle finger, stretching skin forward. Smiles — nervously. "I was scared." He lost his fishing gear but can buy things again.

         Protecting the back of his neck from the sun
          Black Baseball Cap pushes a wide barrow,
           ferries pineapples beyond the screen.

    Coals scurry, rats round a tin plate,
flicking heat dots.
"Given the unbelievable price of tobacco ..."
    Black Sweatshirt slap-slaps cards with palm,
nails the cracks in the system.

10:30

a low, pink light. To a washed wood table mother and other child arrive.
Daughter hangs her cream leather bag on the back of a freshly painted chair,
clears her throat, getting ready to talk into the Reuters mic.
Father shuffles sideways between table and wall, squeezes next to her,
who says that they do have a little hope, just to find Erika's body.

>The house where Francesco lives
>has a grand arch.
>The house where Francesco lives
>has a wide postbox
>for many, many letters which say
>>"Go back on board," or
>>"I will make you pay for this."
>
>Blue van shuffles, embarrassed
>to be parked so close
>to such a fool of a captain.

12:45

over him with a thin, white sheet.
                                      Sssshhh.
Don't look at his chest hairs
                                      stiff with dried blood.
Wheel the shrouded flesh,
                                      stir the morgue's rickety music
of trolley wheels.
Booth-photo of pursed lips and pepper-salt beard
                                      smiles as his coffin slides down into dry earth,
muffling the next voice crossed off the hitlist.

Moving down the page,   she caught rumours of regulation.
                  Wikipedia   has   gone   dark.
          The student turns to the newsfeed of Facebook, and scrolls
                                                        down
       to mind-taste her friend's last bento.

       A dog watches from a window.
       Neighbours observe from their balcony
              Tamalis,
                  who rocks her baby in her wobbly chair
                  in the house in a bad state.

18:12

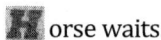orse waits.

Horse waits.

Horse waits.

Man enters on motorbike under arch.

"We shall start again." He tries,
"Climb down the friendly ladder."
The fireman lifts her from the wreck
whose walls can only smoulder.

We'll tell you more later.

Laughter rolls around the *Casa del Migrante*.
Jeans squeeze together on hard floor
hoping, later, to catch a train across the border .
A young woman tries on a brown jacket by the sign,
ropa mujer. Cabbage stew slops into paper bowls.
One lady pulls her sweatshirt sleeve down.
She has slightly hurt her arm
trying to leap onto the carriage ladder.
She turned back, shook her head: "Not this time".

Mid of frozen, glutinous rice balls

These hills always had snow, which melted down into rivers.
Where has it gone?
Our pots of beans bubble.
Even *tesguino* and peyote can't drag us through drought.

Mid of frozen cucumber

A boy patrols his beach:
"The fish die, you can't swim."
Yellow helicopter hovers like a kestrel.
Dauntless dog sprawls in the ripples.
Spilt oil slips closer.

Mid of woman shovelling coal into pot

We tie Choco-Pies to condom-esque balloons,
release packs into pasty sky with leaflets
that say **Down with the dictatorship**.
They meander in teams across the border.
One volunteer rips open a scarlet wrapper.
She giggles, keeping a hand over her chewing.

She yelps like a monkey, all of a sudden.

21:11

Poor because of you!

Cardboard protests make their point
                          above handwritten breasts.

Poor because of you!

The B-movie tigress yanks a gate
                          which doesn't open.

The joy of being a young policeman is so great,
                          he laughs,
as ladies tunnel between his navy trousers.

    Bilal holds a nail in his palm.

    He squats, shows bullet heads

    scattered from sniping.

    Coats on cycles exeunt down an alley

    beneath scribble on crumbling walls:

Free Army, defeater of Assad

He sips coffee behind sandbags,

rifle at ease.

      "Now friends, this is strictly symbolic — Our candidate must be
                      someone who can instinctively
                              turn right."

A bright morning outside the Palace of Culture.

Women walking to work warm their hands cupping coffee.

At a bus stop, a boy clutches a scarf to sensitive teeth.

The grass is hard.

He crunches down slope

with shovel and pickaxe

and hacks a seam in dogged effort

to keep his family from freezing.

One bucket can't last long.

"If we do this to have coal to burn,

would we reject paying work?"

    Brittle ice-fingers,

    fractured by hammer-hull

    re-knit in quiet behind the bow.

Stopping the van on a forest road, stiff fingers set pine on fire to thaw thoughts. Behind 68's rusty number, between curtains of icicles, convection lifts family photographs taped to pink flock wallpaper. Stroke my cat to keep warm.
    More logs please.

23:50

they were confused, wondering,
where have the people gone?
Then our friends began to turn away in scorn
despite our offerings. Like this ostrich.
Problem is it's quick.
We follow it down the street in our Toyota.
It ambles before the bumper.
It will not rush,
reminding us of a schoolboy shuffling home. Then suddenly it's off.
Luckily our day is not wasted.
We net a dog spotted snoozing beneath a bush.

Coming

00:50

I sprinkle maize flour on mother's bed, tease her dry curtains,

prepare walnuts for guests after forty days of soup.

      A carnival bride and groom traipse the gully,
      Calf on roof suckles sunshine from the dug of the west wind.
      A boy's stomach
            spirals
      as men hit tambourines.
Bet you can't clobber a coin with pocket-soft nuts.

When we were wading
            up to our waists,
                  pushing her back into the deep,
      we found what it was to fail
      so we pushed harder until finally
            she floated.
                You can hear me yell
above the rattle of wind on the mic,
      keeping time with my team,
           while Steve explains what we did
                and how we did it, to the reporter.
Gilding a work-free
      worn hand
      with a soft brush, silver hoops flanking her
      wire spectacles,
           Yamila balances up a ladder,
              as she strokes light stripes onto Mary's
           stone robe.
Her husband crouches behind
           cheeks of
           cherubs peeking behind folds.
      His torch tickles the virgin's chin.

03:05

Once, clients forced prostitutes in Osaka
to munch giant sushi rolls for a laugh.

The owner of the 64-year-old tub
spreads the ancient fat on his pumpernickel, nods,
"*Das schmeckt gut!*"
His wife nods: "Yes. It does smell good."
He twizzles the can in-between his fingers,
and she can't help laughing
for the lard is whiter than war-winter,
more *köstliche* than *kuchen*,
a creamy adventure bound up in rusty metal.
The contents of a CARE package snuggled into Berlin
sustained their marriage through the city-siege;
One blue tartan tin looked so *schön*, he kept it.
    Swift's Bland Lard.
    A taste of reconciliation.

07:42

When I think about Guinea I want to send my family a sack of *Riz Jaune*.

I enjoy sweet potatoes but I'm not shopping for myself.

I'm not buying aubergine or oil in a 'Captain's Gin' bottle

as I have done on a sunny half-day in Conakry.

My coffee stays warmish as twilight defines spidery trees.

I wrap my scarf-stripes about my exiled neck

in the *Gamin de Paris*, and click Pay.

    It was a mistake.

    The protocol was followed.

    Warning shots.

    One

    Another.

AMBULANCE is written backwards –

08:55

"Be strong for the old man."

Children swinging on a tyre

will not know Mandela as their president.

Rabbit skins cure, hanging

in the leather worker's shop.

The wind whispers to the hospital ward,

    "Madiba, we need you."

"Grandma are you alive? Did you freeze to death?"

She chuckles and extends her feet forward.

Black dogs circle, barking at the axe which swings

back over the woodcutter's head and arcs down to split logs.

She wriggles her toes:"I think I should vote for Putin.

When I turn on my TV I look at him all the time."

He sinks deeper and deeper into the mud.

I, powerless, stroke his filthy flanks.

My bare calf leans across his strong back.

My toes, his hooves, side by side.

His shoulders must be heaved up

and chestnut flesh dragged,

scraping across silver carborundum.

His rockpool eyes slide

quiet as a butterfish through shadows.

Fifty black pots broil in the open.

Mutton and water. Boys and men

stirring the *kurban*. Mutton and water.

Men and boys topping the *kurban*.

Mutton and water. More and more water.

Summoned by steam, families appear.

Shocking pink candyfloss, tiny tongues

dissolve sugar threads in rosy saliva.

Summons by steam, mutton and water.

Prayers for rain in steady rain.

Veneer in my office. The old flag is made new.

Where are the politicians, may god bless them?

They only come when they have a budget.

I'm waiting in walls with holes, within holes in holes.

      Daughter dances for camera.

I chop tomatoes into blue plastic bowl.

It's a good sharp knife.

      It won't be easy for my children,

born and brought up in Khartoum,

to go back with me to Southern Sudan.

Government TV... "I have just talked to the Commandante and he had a victorious voice. He was having soup, and this made him have an energetic voice! Smile."

      PHONER: "This morning I had yoghurt, and I will be having squash soup after my walk."

10:09

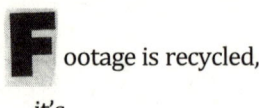ootage is recycled,

    it's

        always

            the

                same.

    The dead plane slipped in suds,

   slid through the cloud,

thudded, soapy

on woodland floor.

    Wet –

    showers through the night –

    running in red pants and vest –

        yeeeeah!

        Heeyaeaaeah!

    Blokes can be blond too!

Passports, papers, pens.

Lines, stamps, fingers.

  Turquoise tiles,

    eloquent calligraphy.

      Burgundy nylon jacket.

              Brave young words

                from a student voter.

        Translation for viewers:

              "I want to blind the enemy."

13:34

First morning light flings cobalt shadows on peach walls.

Snipers bob like seagulls, shooting at hacks abandoning Atarib

at a speed measured in calm panic by a Northern Irish accent.

The vehicle comes to rest by the old olive-garden;

trees silhouetted in sunlight;

        gunfire

        plays.

    This is purported to be Rastan.

    These are children.

    These are victory signs.

                Listen.

    That's cheering.

    And that sound,

    dark and stubby

    is a missile hitting

                directly below the human voice.

Tears roll down tracks of cheeks into open pink mouth.

Facebones ache from unwanted, uncontrollable hiccups.

My twelve-year-old is carried high.

Oh wow, she suddenly shot up, much taller than her mum.

                          White lilies

                          Daffodils

                          Chrysanthemums

When she was walking home from market, seven men jumped.

                    Fifty camels were offered for her silence.

                    She refused and had to leave her father's house.

                          This hospital paint: radioactive green.

If your balcony sides have mostly vanished in shelling, it's sensible to stand outside your flat with a hammer. Try to knock off the most dangerous bits.

14:37

t's going to be a bumper harvest this year.

We will bring in more coffee than in 2010, more than in 2011.

    Don't think all news from our country is bad.

        A cow lows,

                mooo ooo oo.

    Soon it will be dark.

    A crowd of bats fly close by the camera.

Shadows are gathering by the high wire fence,

preparing to move.

Some mothers paint their nails

with a clear polish from a tiny glass vial.

        Even when a son sits in prison – we're not sure which one –

                waiting to be killed, this mother

                      does not bite the ends.

15:42

an pulls hood down and

zips across street

tiptoes beneath satellite dishes, grey fox in grey light.

**intentional
neologism?**

Infants shuffle from

one foot to another.

Parents hang placards round small necks:

**Patience Bashar,
the son of the Kurd
will dig your grave.**

Death has been banned.

Our commune cannot afford you space.

Our deceased will never travel down the road

to be buried over the hill.

That village is full of enemies.

One girl in a cardigan doesn't care

because she is never going to die.

Dark blue and green underpants

sing on the wire of the exile's flat.

Round and round drove the businessman,

round and

round and straight

into Piraeus harbour.

17:56

Six children and one affair later,

her feet were gripped in the stocks

along with those of her lover:

                        Articles of Law: Indigenous Autonomy

17 counts of premeditated murder.

    "Certainly, from what I've read,

there's very little evidence of a crime.

It's fascinating from a defence lawyer's position.

Prove it."

                – goodbye –

        to the void to the dead air buzz

      Trans-logistic knocks for your uranium

18:00

he monkey in the MRI machine fixes on *The Good,*

          the Bad and the Ugly in

     TECHNISCOPE TECHNICOLOR.

    Head secured by screws, monkey brain glistens on the screen.

  He chews, as if he's got a mouthful of gum or popcorn

or cheroot. Actor grabs gun.

    Monkey eyes gleam.

    My dog is sick, so we dress her

      in a party frock. It's her fifteenth birthday.

        Our dog's leg was busted with a machete.

      We ask Saint Lazarus to restore it.

Her dog is lifted up and passed over heads

to the pauper's statue.

        Bewildered eyes

        long for

        the floor.

19:15

eporter in flak jacket

points to a body bathed in

blue light from the night bar,

> whispers,

>> "We're the first crew to arrive, not even police or ambulance is here yet. The victim is still lying on the ground."

A couple of barflies

milling about in

> flip flops

get too close to the groaning.

Yellow Tee-shirt saunters up

to the flailing arms

puts a gun to the terrified head.

> Scene freezes.

>> OoOoOoOoOoOoO

Streets bounce,

houses lurch.

> Later the reporter walks back to the body.

> The medics should arrive soon.

"But really, she shouldn't have been doing that."

The white-haired neighbour rolls her eyes:

> "In the kitchen with the gas-cooker on, apparently."

>> *The lady was decanting petrol into a glass container.*

North Yorkshire duty desk parks the reports adding,

> "It was tea-time at the property."

19:20

Baby dolphins are sprinkled, attracting birds,

who penetrate beak-tubes into rotting innards.

Biologists dissect the gnarled earhole, the curlicue brain

to present samples to the young women who have cycled here

writing elegant tyre glyphs for the sky to decipher.

                The cream soil,

                    the slippage of atmosphere —

        He brandishes the megaphone over his head,

        transmitting warnings from his motorbike:

                "Get out! Time to go!"

        My neighbour jounces to the hills,

            the three dogs she has had since puppies sticking by her.

                      I am a retired banker. Looters may rob my house,

                                so I will wait until 4.30pm

                                      and then

                            then if the sea retreats, I'll run.

"I'm scared to take my wife outside because she dresses like a Muslim."

Bienvenidos a Vilacamba	feeds the white chicken
spreads coffee in sunshine **Isla de la longevidad**	
donde el tiempo	gently sweep porch
damp mist morning	***se detiene y la vida se alarga***
I gather beans	my daughter on my back.
City shoe-wearers	do none of this
They live with machines	in the brand new bungalows
in the Valley	of Long Life.

20:45

"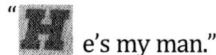e's my man."

                She sucks her lips and

                                grimaces/smiles.

Thumbs up.

                The studio audience laugh and

                                clap,

    knowing where she's coming from,

        i.e. the White House.

21:15

H e is licking

    water droplets

        off a rubber tube.

        Suddenly it's raining in the desert.

    Hope is evacuating from a tanker parked on salmon powder

        onto the face tilted towards the chassis.

            As the boy stands beneath the truck

                water crows out of the ripped steel.

Soldiers on the skyline

occupy outposts

        sunken in thought.

22:31

1.

Lying shivering, seeing friends make moves

they shouldn't do, ducking, dodging.

                                    He comes out of the wood.

One by one he shoots them all. One by one they topple.

                                    It's so hushed.

I feel him place his boots right in front of my face

                                    – the warmth of the barrel.

Loud bang. Like being punched in the shoulder.

                                  I try to keep it at a distance.

2.

Seeing the place I saw the killing

felt – well –

as I stepped off the boat

I moved one pace closer

to taking this island back.

22:54

n o F1 visas for Reuters this year.

        The stench of blistering rubber is searing Manama.

        The man sweeps his T-shirted arm and his team

        arrange wide tyres, slosh gasoline, prop an upturned-up bin

        and whack a water tank onto the end.

Small crews are lighting car parts at junctions

on deserted village roads encircling the capital.

Armoured vans crouch on the dustside.

        "Help me. Help me. Help me."

            A hand reaches out of

                the black slick,

    scrabbles, and

    slips back into

the greasy pit.

        On hands and knees, painted to the waist,

           lanced with pica, meet Toro.

           Toro points the pica at Toro

           ripping energy from pavement slabs.

    Toro is tiny and roosts on a hat —

                    Bulls suffer!

        Put your heart deep down inside the skin of a bull.

        The young weep because animals are hurt.

The whole enchilada grinds to a halt, eventually.

Even the attitudes of generations.

What would she look like aged nine? How would her hair be cut?

The artist has reconstructed the kind of school photo

she wouldn't show friends

        if she has grown older.

People get ready to resound with a caring song, a Marxist song.

Older voices of the rainbow singsong with the high pitched children.

Locked in the courthouse the villain can't listen to his serenade.

The crowd whistles in the rain, harmonising words that he says

have brainwashed millions. What does he feel about this?

"He's not a man of many reactions," remarks his defence lawyer.

    One blue sky above us

    One ocean lapping our shore

    There's no shortcut to freedom

23:16

ver the crest of cornstalk bundles,

the reporter gets a limited view

of an activist's yard.

By lifting his chin and lengthening his neck

he can spy Chen and son making tea.

Chen	and	as	Bamboo
shifts	beyond	a	is
from	the	silver	bending
foot	television	cat	
to		darts	
foot,		between	
shuffles		his	
round		sandals.	
his			
couch			

like the reconstruction artist who climbs into a bag to see if it's possible to zip and lock himself in. He pulls the sides over himself, but what a struggle, elbows and knees don't fit. He twists and turns and soon his head disappears underneath red showerproof cloth. He manages eventually but this is only after he moves out of the bath onto the lounge floor. Perhaps it's easier there.

Bear goes to university.

Not having paid his fees

he loses his grip

on the thick branch

and must

                    tumble

             through the canopy.

       Hear the campus shriek

as he thuds

onto a safety pad.

         He's licking his saliva

           dripping on the mattress

         from his pink, curly tongue.

       It's comfier to wear sunglasses when priming a rifle in this sun.

He sets up his laptop

                  on the coca cola fridge.

Double megaphones —

      Tell me how you feel driving this land,

          are you all right?

We could cut it up into tiny pieces, yes.

Beyond

00:12

*t*he protestors try to get into the *souk* to see tourists. "Oh why don't you respect your royalty like the people of England respect their queen?" asks the riot cop. The daughter of the hunger striker grins, preparing for a crunch.

        eyeliner

        powder

        brush

        perfume in a glass dome

        foundation cream

        yellow lid

        blue lid

        brush attached to compact with rubber band

These treasures belong to a daughter who loved her work

as a flight attendant.

    "She never took a day off. She worked tirelessly."

The car butts onto the trottoir.

                          Cheeky.

How could he have thought the metro was a car park

      with those art nouveau railings?

          Bikes cluster, sniggering.

        How does a journalist lie?

      In a ditch, heels in the water.

How does a journalist die?

        Secretly.

             A swollen stomach, green

      T-shirt pulled up.

    Grab well-fed arms.

Pull this lump to the top.

If you draw lines in day-glo on the crossword in the national paper,

they highlight an evil code planning the assassination of the brother of Chavez:

      Kill

             Gunfire

       Adan.

Two blokes chat on phones, tums drooping off the galvanised booths.

      The boy would prefer to sleep in a sewage pipe

        than on a

             veranda,

      because if he did that the owners

      might think he was going to rob them.

     Tabletop football pitch bolted to his screwball bike —

     no one cares if crazy old Didi cycles on the pavement.

Le peuple Winneba du Ghana chasses l'antilope selon un rite ancien.

Slumped over sweaty shoulders, secured by ankles and front legs, the gazelle frolics up and down.

     seesaw yoyo vacillating rhythm

An angry caterpillar or Chinese lion celebrating new year.

           trrrrrrrrrrrrrr oh oh

The procession cantillates forward.

                              shimmy, step, stride by step step

Now the deer has given up.

                          Birthday

                 cake for Buddha.

           Stupas surrounded by colour.

         Novices bow in flowing apparel.

        Then they go off to play football.

02:25

T in   neighbourhood.
Tin   in heat.
Worms in Adam's ale
                        wriggled from factory.
Rust   devours stopcock.
A cut-off bottle dangles on wire
off wood ----------
------x------------x----------
--- x --- that was the door blown open by the wind.

      I'm Citta, an elephant
and I'm selecting one melon out of three.
One's for Poland, one's for Greece,
the other means it's a draw.
      I'm from Ukraine; a friendly pig.
What a sweet and charming face. That's me!
I snuffle my nose through bars.
Oh — and I'm psychic.

      A strike on militants you say?
      Even I can see that's a dead baby.
          A village is gone now
          and the empty wheelbarrow
          looks so bloody
                    pointless.

03:27

Get the monster out of Lady Gaga!

"I hope people realise we are not angry with her,

only at her blasphemy — Lady Gaga, you are not beyond repentance."

It's dark. A rain flurry smacks hymn-singers' umbrellas.

The anti-riot police would get drenched, except they have plastic shields.

> When the girl jives in short black skirt she points down to the floor and sticks her bottom out. Hey, she's cool, really attractive, and maybe North Koreans aren't so bad after all. "They have lovely skin — clean and fresh", cries a young woman on a bench in front of the screen at Seoul Central Station.

>We don't want to live here any more.

>The green isn't green enough.

>>Horse's white bones

>>yaw into an awning for locusts.

06:35

If my father was not a good coach, I would be married by now. This is how it was for me. I wore tracksuit and T-shirt, not *salwar kameez*. We can't afford a wrestler's mat, and an athlete's diet, milk and vegetables, costs. If I was late for one minute, I would get the stick, but at least I was excused household tasks for *kushti*. (Her mother pours water over her baby, the black buffalo, rubbing his hairy chops.) Geeta has wrestled her sisters in yards of mud in mud-yards prepping for her debut in East London.

06:48

T he politicians embrace
        the delicate figurine for the press shot
but don't actually touch her,
        thinking that she could break
or that it is not right
        to make contact with a saint.
A prime minister's wife
        grabs a queen by the waist.
They roll up the stairs,
        away from the silver light,
fringed shawls frisking
        like sheepdogs.
The lady says
        in her soft contralto
that she feels she has known
        Akershus Castle a long time.
In the setting sun, beneath trees
        that think, guards straddle piebalds.

                                            Said to be Houla.
                              Unable to verify independently
                                  who is screaming Allah,
                            or whose face is covered in blood.

                Winds of hope,
                wings of worry.

        "I don't know when I might pass away,

     but until then

   I want to live life without any regrets."

"I used to wish she would meet a good partner,

but I don't think that was very effective.

Now I don't care whether it is a good match.

I simply want her to marry,"

    a mother's words beaten into gold tongues.

      Fires smoulder

          where houses

                crumbled.

Instant archaeology.

    Through the ashes

        creep giant   insects in shirts

          who gather

        to fire bullets at aircraft:

   "We are still here, you bastards."

07:13

The child's arm is the bit not trapped under the bus.

His yellow wristband, fastened on its third hole, shines pale as a primrose.

        How many rebels can

              climb onto a tank

                      to hug for a

                              yearbook photo?

                                      Loose metal clink slips,

                    whee scree,

                as young men scramble

        to the top

      to the turret.

A bandaged hand — left-eye salutes!

Come on guys, big kiss for a brother in a stripy T-shirt.

        She wheels onto the moving staircase, which as it rises, tips

            her chair backwards and over she goes, and then over

                again back down, cheek debossing

                    on metal ridges. The man

                      who rushes to help,

                        trips.

            She drinks porridge from a tin cup,

                staring into the lens — jumps

                    as she misses her mouth

              and a huge slurp lands on her lap.

14:30

not enough workers to run Olympic security?

Thank goodness the army can step into this humiliating gap.

Committee laughs.

I promise to bring back prestige, dignity

and anything that will make Somalis happy.

Together to victory in my emotional Games!

                        Latex

            gloves   extend the python on the slab

            and intersect her side with a sterile knife

                    to wrap fingers around   eggs

                bloody with unbirth.

                        Behold

                        eighty-seven

                potential invaders of the Everglades,

                        each flexible case semi-opaque,

                              shell-slippy in

                                    mucus.

I'm so disappointed with these bad debts —

       the deficit and the economy.

On this aircraft carrier, I tell you,

           sport doesn't make me forget money.

                A ginger sheep sleeps in the valley,

                the little thing's dead, so it is.

                He points to a chasm in her side.

                          She went quickly.

15:45

exual health low?

                    Upgrade with a nifty salad.

                    Freckle walnuts on baby leaves.

Why not   dribble crumbs on vanilla cream

                                    wobbling in a ramekin,

or   sprinkle specks onto towers

                                    of mini-pancakes?

Horse. The Dry One. M-13. Mara Salvatrucha.

Rabbits. Buffalo horns.

Everyone is born with a puppet that sprouts a long yellow nose and red lips,

                    or maybe one that looks more like themselves.

If you chopped a piece of wood you might uncover a face

        sticking its tongue out at your ideas,

a mouse dancing badly,

                            a bad bull sprouting moonhorns,

            a lion, a cow, a high-toed antelope.

I do not have money.

My puppets will be my future.

17:58

igns over chopping boards.

Hand   signs over coffee

Hands shovel fava beans.

Consuming customers

                 savour jaws closing,

                             chomp and chomp,

                             tongues licking teeth,

                             throats slurping water

       while cooks and waiters

       get on with their jobs

               in Gaza's first deaf restaurant.

Glancing at camera, grey coughs racking the last days at work,

boots tramp on ochre leaves he'll be scrunching forever.

       shocked

               Yes

The manager had trouble moving his mouth through his final speech.

Tiny hens peck open seams of Candeleros Formation.

Sandstone, windblone,   **I assume that**

silstone, hill-grown.   **these are**

Eolion paleson,   **deliberate neologisms?**

Mesozoic, cretaceous.

The early Cenomanian

hid in ossified outcrops with her best friends,

a scratching squirrel and a snake with feet.

Bongos!

        Bongos!

                Expo-Weed.

A rolled-up leaf, lightly gripped between lace-edged teeth

        and a bottom lip,

                The inhale is cruel and unforgiving. Rasp.

    V for victory.

        Victory of the weed within society. Victorious.

Sitting in circles of solidarity.

                There,

            here,

         over there,

      there.

A dog dances between groups.

22:58

Equipment and protective clothes
have been smuggled in from Egypt down tunnels —
for paintball. Shoot!

Rooftops are breeding fish
and buoyant faeces fertilise peppers
for a healthy market.

What? A warning shot you say?
Perhaps exploding early morning
— disengagement and mortar.

Multiple strikes, new war.
Targeted car, armed wing.
Coastal enclave, Hamas radio,

hello, who is this?

Battle

11:59

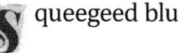queegeed blue it's true.

    It's too good for you.

  A fiery lob trails across.

Interception.

    The Iron Dome knocks out a rocket on its way to Tel Aviv.

      The TV car is driving on the

          pavement because in the road

              another car is on fire.

Ashkelon residents are fleeing for cover.

    On the roof, a tank

        pukes out entrails.

      Homes groan, disembowelled.

A head of cabbage is up —

six or seven shekels.

There's a shortage of antibiotics.

What have we got?

    Only stones and only sticks.

The stadium is billowing,

attacked by armed hecklers.

        More of skyline.

        More of skyline.

More of

some indications of a truce ahead

> The scent of victory trails after long-legged M-75, flashing into Israel.
>
> We called our new range of orange perfume after the super-rocket.
>
> Living in a siege you often can't get the real thing so we knock out knock-offs.

12:01

akwa-Ibom percolates yellow into sickly soil.

Headless flowers and stems sweat in crude oil.

    He scoops slurry into a pan, the thick black juice

  is to power cars but in lake is no use:

      "We are hungry

        and will spend New Year hungry."

              Splash!

        Man tips bucketfuls over fence.

              Splash!

          Amber alert — serious rain.

              Splash!

Gumboots pushing wheelbarrows — more sacks.

              Splash!

Squash sandbags down — wearing Wellingtons.

              Splash!

        Woman tips bucketfuls over fence.

              Splash!

        Dog tips bucketfuls over cat.

The Eye Witness News van

parks outside the hospital

    where crystalline concretions,

        bile-grown olive and umber calculi,

formed in prison and in government,

    are removed.

                    The International Treasure's

            admixture of calcium and bilirubin

    proves more priceless than

                            rare diamonds.

To keep warm, keep moving. Snow is exhausting.
It would be so much easier to tuck up inside a snow
duvet and dream. They are forced to run in circles
about a burning trailer to stay awake. To keep warm,
keep moving. Their ears throb in red, raw waves
as the blood pumps pum pum down the red alleys.
To keep warm, keep moving. The two freezing
elephants are forced to glug vodka with tepid water
before being led to a school gym to be examined.
Frostbite on pinnae and nose, could be worse.
The pair have reached Omsk and have started rehearsals,
walking round and around. No audience. Slowly round,
turning around indoors. To keep warm, keep moving.

        JPL and Lockheed Martin Grail orbiters,

                            Ebb and Flow

            smash land on a far place.

        Machines have journeyed

                space-leagues

    to show us

                contours of craters,

    to map

            our dark moonface.

13:29

Dallas Whippy tells us his house overturned at 4pm.
His toilet collapsed on its side, a bent stamen
as the house unfolds its salmon orange wallpetals.
Vantaged above tarmac road, lads straddle an inclined palm
brandishing machetes from their impossible horse.

Crystals on the road, tossed in the troposphere — wheee eee!
Fur-wrapped, junior professionals tug each other along on sledges.
They're scoffing hot nuts, oily slicks on nail varnish.
A little snow, it's enough.
Small snow men.
Quiet snow men.
Hush-hush in the blank.
    Soon the vicious rape of a paramedic
        shall explode the silence.   **"will"?**

He peels the tupperware lid back to broadcast folded pancakes.
Meat cutlets and apple pies, requested via Twitter, hum in his bag.
His wife's sewing group has been embroidering police badges.
There's a cold snap. Prison clothes can't be enough in Nordovian cells.

14:33

                                          comet.
                              primitive
                   a
           tracks
Onlooker

                         He notes the sticky glare

                         the gods call the Greek Fire.

                    It ignites muscles.

                Day after day the angry glue

          plummets further inside arms

          baking delicious marrow.

      Napalm, thermite, white phosphorous.

      Bad birds on black winds,

streaming thin chalky smoke;

he writes of this in his book.

Late Cretaceous marine aquatic, fossil primitive,

juvenile *pannoniasaurus mosasaur*.

One summer she was swimming upriver to mate.

15:22

ittle girl, are you scared of the end of the globe?
    Tell father of your fears.
He can build concrete spheres,   "a concrete sphere"?
    line its contours with blossom-paper.
He can rig up power from gas and generator
    and plant private gadgets.
When your ball-house bounces,
    a seat belt will strap you down safely.
An oxygen tank will inspire you
    to keep taking deep, innocent breaths.
You shall fly on risen floodwater.
Preserved seed — intact inside your nut-case
    you will bob through flickering mist,
    weave west on cutting seas of grey earth
        out into virgin sunny daze, you will discover land,
        deposited on a placental mountain.

It's better to be prepared for nothing
than to be unprepared for something.

    An assassin slashed.
A Eye of Horus poked into his throat
healed the gash, helping king-man-god
to obtain his allotted after-life.
    Unknown 'E', unembalmed,
enveloped in goat's skin,
stunk out this dry tomb.
A man forced to hang himself here?

    Microscopes reveal a second son.

The base notes of expectation

deafened his ears,

he always came second.

    Rotting malodour,

no hieroglyphic favour.

A dished body slumped

without prayers, no forever;

    buried dying.

We need candles. Rush out to the shops for

the 21st will be followed by three

days and nights too

of the one

d

a

r

k

.

In the 'last sun' ritual, Baby's feet skitter in a final cycle.

The end of calendars.

0

The start of calendars.

A multicultural world. Love lagoons, respect mountains.

  Michael Coe in the 1960s said that 2012 could herald an "Armageddon to cleanse humanity" *From the Olmecs to the Aztecs,* (1962, sixth edition, 2008) - with Rex Koontz.

Police-pelican shores.

Ceremonies ward off calamity.

Rub flowers on Bolon Yokte —

                                        wind will unhurry.

Let flow water on Neptune —

                                        sea will unruffle.

Incas won't believe the Maya.

Our magic will foil their End of the World.

We came here for the fun of the story;

same as the journalists,   we came here

to meet some crazy people.

17:50

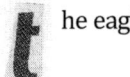he eagle

                                        swoops

                    to snatch a baby

from right under her mother's unsuspecting smile.

The raptor

                                    yanks

              the 3D child into the air.

It's only a model. Just shows you though, doesn't it?

The fire in the tent prepares the fighters.

An army is brewing closer to an airport.

Jeans don't really keep you warm with a short jacket.

You tread slowly trying not to slip and lose your plastic bag of shopping.

White stallions have redecorated a metal fence in salty icicles

lace-making, and washing on a balcony has dripped into draped stone.

Fair play to the two mares drawing a cart down a very long lane.

In sweltry streets, marketeers shift tins of honeycomb that cracks.

Tepid honey oozes out, lava-fresh, "The best in the world."

Break off a segment of comb and it's your tongue that unfurls.

Pick up the skinny strip of wood, drones scraping so near

that bees brush your fingers with leg hair.

20:41

        queueing down the stride of Madrid's boulevards,

            desperate to play the Christmas lottery:

                      the Fat One.

Santa blows kisses from a cable car, cruising the steep slope to Sugarloaf,

        boogies round the peak, la-la-ing jingle bells.

Ding ding ding

      Coriander oilseed island palace

            but at Kota Zoo, the table

        bears bodies of five pregnant females.

                  Instruments probe the bodies.

Hmm — a lung infection.

Was it water?

Was it feed?

        Why did a bounce of blackbucks spring over the river?

If a man is careless,

if he doesn't care about his city,

if he doesn't care about cleanliness,

if he spits without self-discipline ...

yes.   There are issues.

      But I am not to blame for his careless behaviour.

We stallholders have, since days of the evil kings,

wrapped nuts in folded leaves on our well-kept trolleys

parked on the verge for the convenience of travellers and workers.

                    I'm looking at the filthy crud.

       Red stains radiating up

                                    the peeling walls,

          as if pigeons have been shot

                                          in the urinals.

It's not our fault, we only sell the stimulant

which is also an antiseptic.

20:55

The old pink scooter tows a trailer of garden produce past the monument. Hunching in a headscarf a woman hands out information on A4, saying, "When we all die, no one will remember us." After the statue was ousted to applause at least one man thumped the air and another went round the ear and slapped Josef's hard, cold head with the flat of his hand.

Back in 1904, Cromwell Wall addressed the phonograph,

fine-tuned his starched collar, and pronounced,

"Christmas is a Season of Goodwill. Families come first."

Installing the thingamabob in a pram he uphilled the oiled wheels

onward over the wobbly cobbles of Friern Barnet

to secure the bells of Old Southgate tintinnabulating at midnight

for his great-grandchildren:

        Old Gramophone Speed 132

        New Gramophone Speed E.2

"This happened after the revolution." A professor gestures to stacks of plastic junk built-up in front of the Red Sea. An expert in political sociology he opines on land rights. Goats graze. A girl tugs a nanny's ear.

A camel, be-pompommed, toddles through a shady gate to register at the Hilton Hotel.

21:31

After kneading, moulding she paddles the dough with the criss-cross bat and glazes the lattice. Her glove shuffles the shelf beneath jets of gas. So many *khalija*, and boxes of tins of *khalija* packed up to go on the Nissan pick-up. Shooting out beneath black cloth her hands jot an order in her pad.

That was in Saudi Arabia; whereas in Kashmir a drummer (Farah) plays open-handed in the first girl group to rock the valley. Their guitarist and bassist boing, lambs in sports shoes; their frontwoman croons into a Shure. The band shoe-gaze, leaning generally towards the attentive greywool heads of young men attending **Battle of the Bands 2012**.

22:19

One's her own,   one's her mother's;

      a little girl's mismatched shoes

                lift her bare toes off unpleasance.

    Scarves swish round ladies

who once shopped in merchant-rich Aleppo.

              Can't make a fire because of the rain.

    Two loaves

        don't split into meals for six.

Bum from Kiev has an unfortunate name in English but his concern is that despite

the wood burner, the tent for the homeless loses heat. Bending forward,

Taras Shevenko doffs a cap of white; his snowcape shivers on stone shoulders.

Sons go trudging and fishing on the Dnieper River. Silver tails flick on crystal drifts.

Settlement

07:11

        G irls assist at tea

                    stalls or

           toddle barefoot.

        Mother

     bending,

sweeps.   Boys dandle toy guns.

   Cheery jumpers knit bright patterns: triangles pink,

   stripes lime green... come closer. Nasal passages

   whirr with snot. A line of bench men sip heat

   from glasses. Refugee steam chuffs from a brazier.

Bienvenue.

Trucks trundle up the sandy road.

In a balmy gush from the tyres,

bush grass hardly wavers.

Helicopter surveys the hills,

on the hunt for robbers

who separate faces from elephants.

       Broken bricks bend ankles of rescuers.

09:58

There's something amazing, thinks a shopper shuffling

down concrete streets, about happening on patch of fir trees,

perfume spiky as key lime pie or figs in syrup.

Customers in designer coats stand for only five minutes,

complain, "I'm freezing, hurry up, hurry up I'm freezing.

Come on." Stallholders would like to reply,

"Well, get dressed baby, what are you talking?" **Something missing?**

Last year it was impossible to even enter a store about now.

We're screwed.

If people don't shop coming up to Christmas,

when will they?

On Christmas day last year,

Boko Haram rammed a car

packed with explosives

into the gates of St Theresa's Church, Madalla.

Sixteen-year-old Hope reposes flowers

on her brother's grave,

in a pink T-shirt with the word

Forever.

"I will say at first blush that it appears

it was a trap;

that there was a car in a house,

that it was engulfed in flames.

It was probably set by Mr Spangler

who marked time, sweating,

then shot the first responders."

>Do angels need stockings?
>
>**Noah 6, Jessica 6**

10:37

An anonymous tip-off led to this end-house.
    Prising away its   roof,
    we can discern its   floor
    has been hoarding   shoes,
    old clothes and amassing piles, yes,

                              piles

of buckets by a lightless hole disappearing down.

                Through the ocean.
                        Sneaky.
        The teeth closed in.
      Serrated jaw
    chewed chunks off his leg.
          He slammed the nub of his board
              into the shark's.
      Bandaged on a stretcher,
gives a thumbs-up with his decent hand.

12:11

ed petals, bluey-grey stem

hills on the table — carnations

          to deliver **I'm sorry** and **I love you.**

Men organize flowers

children observe their uncles' labour,

          birds in the eaves of the polytunnel twittering

Happy Birthday to Germany from Gaza.

        If you occasionally buy this product,

        please kindly resend this letter

        to the World Human Rights Organization ...

15:48

Dear Father Frost:

    Please make the writer's parents

    marry again

    and stop quarrelling.

        Fish man from

                18 metre well.

        He tripped in while cleaning,

        gets pulled out to the chorus:

            Happy Holidays!

16:57

It's so impersonal when you can buy your baguette anywhere.

They're closing the *boulangerie* closest to the Louvre.

Paris has far too many sandwich shops and sushi bars.

Assad will not be overthrown predicts a Lebanese fortune teller.

Meanwhile, the Egyptian pound plummets to a record low.

She handled the bones in an unlawful way.

The cupboard behind the rail of suits

concealed the incomplete skeleton.

The *tukuls* burnt down and the health clinic too.

Nothing remained of the village.

Hunger swells since prowlers stole the cows.

Bullet bra cups will never be filled.

19:59

I am Jewish /

I am Jewish /

I am Jewish /

I am Jewish /

put me on that list

this new list

the Jews' list /   **? not sure**

if I am /

if I'm not

put my name at the bottom

or near the top /

        People, I thought we were done with this.

        I kick inside my mother.

        She flops on damp grass, chewing.

        To the barn we go, what's the hurry?

        The tags in her ears are embossed: 6466.

        Lucky for us. The robot slides beneath her

        and sucks.

The threat came by text.

The journalists vow to keep working

despite the targeted killings.

    He hoists his pink shirt to perform his stomach,

    the railroad that tracks down to the groin

    where his skin has knitted back.

20:34

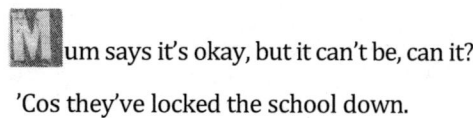um says it's okay, but it can't be, can it?

'Cos they've locked the school down.

Police saw a man

with a gun

and the school say it's better to be safe

than sorry.

I don't want Mum to worry more.

I'll go back.

But I can't concentrate.

21:34

"Oh," says the American teacher, "This is the best day of the year."
Trunk twists behind and over her head to take the doll from a rider
and picks it for a child, like fruit. Other elephants dance, perform handstands

when the waterglass glares like a mouse and the sky is flat cloud,
Glumchild stares at Santa going bum down
as he fails to control his skis on the so-so-cold lake.
The reindeer hoof in and assume charge of the sleigh

if our teams can work out the drift
                               it's floating
                                     loose fay
Tests are underway into confetti.
        believe how its restless falling
in between that measureless gap
which opens
at midnight
        Our plan is to prioritise rooftops.